The Little Book
of Wisdom

Compiled and Illustrated by
Richard Torregrossa

Health Communications, Inc.
Deerfield Beach, Florida

©1996 Richard Torregrossa
ISBN 1-55874-422-3

Publisher: Health Communications, Inc.
          3201 S.W. 15th Street
          Deerfield Beach, Florida 33442-8190

Cover illustration by Richard Torregrossa

This book is dedicated
to Mrs. Joya Torregrossa,
with love and gratitude

Acknowledgments

I am deeply grateful to my friend, Arthur S. Goldwag, for his consistent support, encouragement and editorial insights.

I would also like to thank my sister, Judith Wilson, and her daughter, Christine, for their contributions and encouragement. Thanks, too, to Patty Wilson and Mr. Aviation, John Cameron Bishop, for sending me quotes.

I would also like to thank Anita Carson and Celia Tappia for their help in the early development of this book.

Many thanks to Justine Wenman, graphic designer par excellence, for her Macintosh magic and superb artistic touches.

Thanks to Lilly for help with the cover design.

I additionally owe a debt of gratitude to "the computer boys," Dan "Woody" Woodard and Tom "The Man" Morgan, for their assistance.

And finally, a heartfelt thanks to Steven Kent, my literary agent and advisor, without whom none of this would have seen the light of day.

Introduction

Most collections of quotations are the result of research or some particular process of selection. That's not the case here. These quotations found me, usually at propitious moments, when the last thing on my mind was book work. For instance, I was sitting in the office of a couples counselor, idly flipping through a magazine, feeling somewhat hopeless about the relationship that had brought me there, when I stumbled upon Willa Cather's, "Wherever there is great love, there are always miracles." This short shifted my vantage point just enough to place the moment in a different light. Sometimes that's all you need to feel on top of a situation.

The quotes here have done that for me time and time again, and represent about eight years of such experiences. While this criterion might seem a little personal, I think it can work in the same way for anyone. Pick up this book at different times and let it speak to you.

"The most valuable work you do," goes the quote by P. M. Senge, "may be done in as little as five seconds. . . . A higher vantage point, a brilliant idea, a key change in habit, a break from pressure . . . or a pivotal decision can produce significant, lasting benefits."

Where there is great love there are always miracles.

—Willa Cather
Death Comes for the Archbishop

1

Much better to do your own work, even if you have to do it imperfectly, then to do other people's work perfectly.

—Bhagavad Gita

The Master doesn't seek fulfillment. Not seeking, not expecting. She is present, and can welcome all things.

—Tao Te Ching
Translated by Stephen Mitchell

We make a living by what we get, but we make a life by what we give.

—Winston Churchill

Self-loving is not so vile a sin, my liege, as self-neglecting.

—Shakespeare

Inside every human being is a God in embryo. It has only one desire—it wants to be born.

—Kahlil Gibran

If you are pained by external things, it is
not they that disturb you, but your own
judgment of them. And it is in your power
to wipe out that judgment now.

—*Marcus Aurelius*

Simplicity is the last step of art, and the beginning of nature. Be soft yet not yielding; firm, yet not hard.

—Bruce Lee

In art, as in literature, ugliness rendered with compassion is beauty.

—W. Joe Innis, Artist

There are no coincidences, only fortuitous events.

—Milan Kundera

16

When you do something, you should burn yourself completely, like a good bonfire, leaving no trace of yourself.

—Shunryu Suzuki
Zen Mind, Beginner's Kind

There is no scarcity of opportunity to make a living at what you love; there's only a scarcity of resolve to make it happen.

—Wayne Dyer

A weed is no more than a flower in disguise.

—James Lowell

Never speak of anything concerning yourself which is worthy of praise—such as your learning, virtues, or descent—unless with the hope that some profit will come of it. If you do so speak, let it be with humility and the remembrance that these are gifts from the hand of God.

—*Source Unknown*

The sound of a kiss is not so loud as that of a cannon, but its echo lasts a great deal longer.

—Oliver Wendell Holmes

Intimacy is not fusion or unconditional love or even gratification, but reality and truth of what is.

—Helen Kobai-Yuho Harkaspi
sensei

This is the true joy in life, the being used for a purpose recognized by yourself as a mighty one; the being thoroughly worn out before you are thrown on the scrap heap; the being a force of Nature instead of a feverish selfish little clod of ailments and grievances complaining that the world will not devote itself to making you happy.

—George Bernard Shaw
Man & Superman

For the truly faithful, no miracle is necessary. For those who doubt, no miracle is sufficient.

—Nancy Gibbs

Let nothing be done through strife.

—*Philippians 2:3*

To dream of the person you would like to be
is to waste the person you are.

—*Anonymous*

Success is getting what you want.
Happiness is liking what you get.

—H. Jackson Brown
A Father's Book of Wisdom

To have freedom be willing to give freedom.

—Sanaya Roman
Living with Joy

Through repetition the magic will be forced to rise.

—*Alchemical precept*

Poetry is language at its most distilled
and most powerful.

—Rita Dove

You need not do anything
Remain sitting at your table and listen
Just wait
And you need not even wait, just become
  quiet and still and solitary
And the world will offer itself to you to be
  unmasked
It has no choice
It will roll in ecstasy at your feet.

—Rainer Maria Rilke

Grown men may learn from little children, for the hearts of little children are pure, and, therefore, the Great Spirit may show to them many things which older people miss.

—Black Elk
Native American spiritual leader

A poet looks at the world as a man looks at a woman.

—Wallace Stevens

33

This is a record of your time. This is your movie. Live out your dreams and fantasies. Whisper questions to the Sphinx at night. Sit for hours at sidewalk cafes and drink with your heroes. Make pilgrimages to Mougins and Abiquiu. Look up and down. Believe in the unknown for it is there. Live in many places. Live with flowers and music and books and paintings and sculpture. Keep a record of your time. Learn to read well. Learn to listen and speak well. Know your country, know your world, know your history, know yourself. Take care of yourself physically and mentally. You owe it to yourself. Be good to those around you. And do all of these things with passion. Give all that you can. Remember, Life is short and Death is long.

—Fritz Shoulder
artist

No man ever will unfold the capacities of his own intellect who does not at least checker his life with solitude.

—De Quincey

The best things in life aren't things.

—Art Buchwald

God gives every bird his worm, but he does not throw it into the nest.

—Swedish proverb

Listen to your fear
with a wise ear.
What are you afraid of in life?
What are you afraid of in yourself?
You must challenge fear
and ask it what it means to say.

—Emmanuel's Book
compiled by Pat Rodegast and Judith Stanton

The mind of a perfect man is like a mirror. It grasps nothing. It expects nothing. It reflects but does not hold. Therefore, the perfect man can act without effort.

—Chuang Tzu

Adversity has the effect of eliciting talents which in prosperous circumstances would have lain dormant.

—Horace

Tell me whom you love, and I'll tell you who
you are.

—Creole proverb

We worry about what a child will be tomorrow, yet we forget that he is someone today.

—Stacia Tauscher

To know others is wisdom, to know oneself enlightenment.

—*Tao Te Ching*

45

Whatsoever we beg of God, let us also work for it.

—Jeremy Taylor
English Clergyman (1613-1667)

Take time to be holy.

—Howard Finster
artist and self-proclaimed man of visions

If you help others, you will be helped, perhaps tomorrow, perhaps in one hundred years, but you will be helped. Nature must pay off the debt. . . . It is a mathematical law and all life is mathematics.

—Gurdjieff

The angry man will defeat himself in battle
as well as in life.

—*Samurai maxim*

If you want to kiss the sky you better learn how to kneel.

—U2
"She Moves in Mysterious Ways"

Whenever a fairy tale is told, it becomes night. No matter where the dwelling, no matter the time, no matter the season, the telling of tales causes a starry sky and a white moon to creep from the eaves and hover over the heads of the listeners. Sometimes by the end of the tale, the chamber is filled with daybreak, other times a star shard is left behind, sometimes a ragged thread of storm sky; and whatever is left behind is our bounty to work with, to use toward soul-making.

—Clarissa Pinkola Estes, Ph.D.
Theatre of the Imagination

Words that come from the heart enter the heart.

—The Sages

All you have to do is pause to rest. Nature herself, when we let her, will take care of everything else. It's our impatience that spoils things.

—Jean Moliere

Laughter is inner jogging.

—Norman Cousins

I like trees because they seem more resigned to the way they have to live than other things do.

—Willa Cather

When the sun rises, I go to work,
When the sun goes down, I take my rest
I dig the well from which I drink
I farm the soil that yields my food
I share creation. Kings can do no more.

—Ancient Chinese saying (2500 B.C.)

But now I have learned to listen to silence. To hear its choirs singing the song of ages, chanting the hymns of space, and disclosing the secrets of eternity.

—*Kahlil Gibran*

57

Some of the world's greatest feats were accomplished by people not smart enough to know they were impossible.

—Doug Larson

The library is a temple of learning, and learning has liberated more people than all the wars in history.

—Carl Rowan

Laugh and be fat.

—John Taylor (1560-1684)

Until one is committed there is hesitancy, the chance to draw back, always ineffectiveness. Concerning all acts of initiative and creation there is one elementary truth, the ignorance of which kills countless ideas and splendid plans: that the moment one definitely commits oneself, then providence moves, too. All sorts of things occur to help one that would otherwise never have occurred. A whole stream of events issues from the decision, raising in one's favor all manner of unforeseen incidents and meetings and material assistance, which no man could have dreamt would have come his way.

—G. H. Goethe

Every problem is an assignment from your soul.

—Robin Norwood

He who cannot endure the bad will not live to see the good.

—Yiddish proverb

If no one heeds your call, go forth alone.

—Maharishi Mahesh Yogi

And what a delight to make friends with someone you have despised.

—Colette

Take therefore no thought for the morrow for the morrow shall take thought for the things of itself.

—Matthew 6:34

Flow with whatever may happen and let your mind be free: stay centered by accepting whatever you are doing. This is the ultimate.

—Chuang-Tzu

The smallest thing well done, becomes artistic.

—William Matthews

68

We shall not cease from exploration
And the end of all our exploring
Will be to arrive where we started
And know the place for the first time.

—*T. S. Eliot*

Do the thing and you will have the Power.

—Ralph Waldo Emerson

Everything in nature invites us constantly to be what we are.

—Gretel Ehrlick

Confidence, like art, never comes from having all the answers; it comes from being open to all the questions.

—Earl Gray Stevens

Technical knowledge is not enough. One must transcend techniques so that the art becomes an artless art, growing out of the unconscious.

—Daisetsu Suzuki

Exuberance is beauty.

—William Blake

Our basic nature is to act, and not to be acted upon. As well as enabling us to choose our response to particular circumstances, this empowers us to create circumstances.

—Stephen R. Covey

We have it in our power to begin the world again.

—Thomas Paine, 1732-1809

God's thoughts, His will, His love, His judgments are all man's home. To think His thoughts, to choose His will, to love His loves, to judge His judgments, and thus to know that He is in us, is to be at home.

—George MacDonald

Yesterday is history, tomorrow is a mystery, and today is a gift; that's why they call it the present.

—Source Unknown

78

A little of what you fancy does you good.

—Marie Lloyd

To change one's life: start immediately; do it flamboyantly; no exceptions.

—William James

Properly, we should read for power. Man reading should be man intensely alive. The book should be a ball of light in one's hand.

—Ezra Pound

Music is a higher revelation than philosophy.

—*Beethoven*

All kids are gifted; some just open their packages earlier than others.

—Michael Carr

83

If a June night could talk, it would probably boast that it invented romance.

—Bern Williams

This time, like all times, is a very good time, if we but know what to do with it.

—Ralph Waldo Emerson

The good is one thing; the sensuously pleasant another. These two, differing in their ends, both prompt to action. Blessed are they that choose the good; they that choose the sensuously pleasant miss the goal.

Both the good and the pleasant present themselves to men. The wise, having examined both, distinguish the one from the other. The wise prefer the good to the pleasant, the foolish, driven by fleshly desires, prefer the pleasant to the good.

—Katha Upanishad

One who makes no mistakes, never makes anything.

—Source Unknown

Follow your dream . . . take one step at a time and don't settle for less, just continue to climb.

—Amanda Bradley

Effective interdependence can only be built on a foundation of true independence.

—Stephen R. Covey

Anyone without a sense of humor is at the mercy of everyone else.

—William Rotsler

If a thing loves, it is infinite.

—William Blake

Thus we never live, but we hope to live; and always disposing ourselves to be happy, it is inevitable that we never become so.

—*Blaise Pascal (1632-1662)*

He who would teach men to die, would teach them to live.

—Montaigne

You need even the rocks in the road.

—Ancient Chinese saying

Romance is about the little things.

—Gregory J. Godeck
1001 Ways to Be Romantic

Dare to dream, dare to try, dare to fail—
dare to succeed.

—G. Kinsley Wood

And the wind said: "May you be as strong as the oak, yet flexible as the birch; may you stand tall as the Redwood, live gracefully as the willow; and may you always bear fruit all your days on this earth.

—Native American prayer

He who laughs, lasts.

—Mary Poole

Why scurry about looking for the truth? It vibrates in every thing and every not-thing, right off the tip of your nose. Can you be still and see it in the mountain air? the pine tree? yourself?

—Hua Hu Ching
The Unknown Teachings of Lao Tzu
by Brian Walker

99

Bless, and curse not.

—Romans 12:14

Perpetual optimism is a force multiplier.

—Colin Powell

To love someone is to see a miracle invisible to others.

—François Mauriac

Live simply that others may simply live.

—*Source Unknown*

Wherever you see a successful business, someone once made a courageous decision.

—Peter Drucker

There's no place like home.

—The Wizard of Oz

The love of liberty is the love of others. The love of power is the love of ourselves.

—William Hazlit

A human being is part of a whole, called by us the "universe," a part limited in time and space. He experiences himself, his thoughts and feelings, as something separated from the rest—a kind of optical delusion of consciousness. This delusion is a kind of prison for us, restricting us to our personal desires and to affection for a few persons nearest us. Our task must be to free ourselves from this prison by widening our circles of compassion to embrace all living creatures and the whole of nature in its beauty.

—Albert Einstein

The dogs bark, but the caravan moves on.

—*Arab proverb*

There is a close correlation between getting up in the morning and getting up in the world.

—Ron Dentinger

People are afraid of the future, of the unknown. If a man faces up to it, and takes the dare of the future, he can have some control over his destiny. That's an exciting idea to me, better than waiting with everybody else to see what's going to happen.

—John Glenn

It's never too late to have a happy childhood.

—Source Unknown

Obstacles are what a person sees when he takes his eyes off his goal.

—E. Joseph Cossman

Perseverance is the hard work you do after you get tired of doing the hard work you already did.

—Newt Gingrich

The hardest thing in life to learn is which bridge to cross and which one to burn.

—David Russell

The dogmas of the quiet past are inadequate to the stormy present. The occasion is piled high with difficulty, and we must rise with the occasion. As our case is new, so we must think anew and act anew. We must disenthrall ourselves.

—Abraham Lincoln

$\mathcal{S}$ometimes something worth doing is worth overdoing.

—David Letterman

Have patience with all things, but chiefly have patience with yourself. Do not lose courage in considering your own imperfections, but instantly set about remedying them—every day beginning the task anew.

—St. Francis de Sales

When an ordinary man attains knowledge, he is a sage, when a sage attains under-standing, he is an ordinary man.

—Zen saying

It is very dangerous to go into eternity with possibilities which one has oneself prevented from becoming realities. A possibility is a hint from God.

—Soren Kierkegaard

Great opportunities to help others seldom come, but small ones surround us every day.

—Sally Koch

Go often to the house of thy friend, for weeds choke the unused path.

—Emerson

Better keep yourself clean and bright; you are a window through which you must see the world.

—George Bernard Shaw

In the main it is not by introspection but by reflecting on our living in common with others that we come to know ourselves. What is revealed? It is an original creation. Freely the subject makes himself what he is, never in this life is the making finished, always it is in process, always it is a precarious achievement that can slip and fall and shatter.

—Bernard Lonergan

Intelligence is the effort to do the best you can at your particular job.

—J. C. Penny

You can measure a man by the opposition
it takes to discourage him.

—Robert C. Savage
Life Lessons

Growth is a greater mystery than death. All of us can understand failure, we all contain failure and death within us, but not even the successful man can begin to describe the impalpable elations and apprehensions of growth.

—*Norman Mailer*

The day a person becomes a cynic is the day he loses his youth.

—Marvin D. Levy

The more you depend on forces outside of yourself, the more you are dominated by them.

—Source Unknown

Art is the signature of civilization.

—Beverly Sills

Anyone who stops learning is old, whether at 20 or 80. Anyone who keeps learning stays young. The greatest thing in life is to keep your mind young.

—Henry Ford

Computers are useless. They can only give you answers.

—Pablo Picasso

Let nothing disturb thee;
Let nothing dismay thee;
All things pass;
God never changes.

He who has God
Finds he lacks nothing;
God alone suffices

—Saint Teresa de Cepeda

Are you going places or just being taken?

—H. F. Hendricks

Nurture your mind with great thoughts.

—Benjamin Disraeli

To know you have enough is to be rich.

—Tao

Brightness is more important than cleanliness, because brightness is about the heart, and cleanliness is only about soap!

—Tony Ross
The Shop of Ghosts

136

A friend is a lot of things but a critic he isn't.

—Bern Williams

And you begin to take these things your mind knows and force yourself to live according to them, no matter how comfortable you are, and you say to yourself: "Comfort's not my business; healing is." It is irrelevant that you are tired, uncomfortable and exhausted. Who cares? It is irrelevant. That suddenly no longer has clout. Then these perceptions now have the force to activate your philosophy. Until that time, they are just more and more "warehousing" in your mental field.

—Caroline Myss
Why People Don't Heal

You can't depend on your judgment when your imagination is out of focus.

—*Mark Twain*

Knowledge by suffering entereth; And Life is perfected by Death.

—Elizabeth Barrett Browning

There is no need for temples; no need for complicated philosophy. Our own brain, our own heart is our temple; my philosophy is kindness.

—*The Dalai Lama*

It takes 43 muscles to frown; 17 to smile.

—*Source Unknown*

Before anything else, getting ready is the secret of success.

—Henry Ford

Angels can fly because they take themselves lightly.

—G. K. Chesterton

To do great important tasks, two things are necessary; a plan and not quite enough time.

—*Source Unknown*

You cannot get ahead while you are getting even.

—Representative Dick Armey

All suffering prepares the soul for vision.

—Martin Buber

Intelligence without ambition is a bird without wings.

—C. Archie Danielson

To dissolve fear, turn and look directly at it, for what you face dissolves in the light of consciousness.

—Sanaya Roman
Personal Power Through Awareness

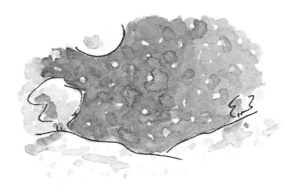

One touch of nature makes the whole world kin.

—Shakespeare

The young do not know enough to be prudent, and therefore they attempt the impossible—and achieve it, generation after generation.

—*Pearl S. Buck*

Control your emotion or it will control you.

—*Samurai maxim*

When one door of happiness closes, another one opens. But often we look so long at the closed door that we do not see the one that has been opened for us.

—Helen Keller

I never got anything that mattered out of my work when it was only something to be exchanged against a pay scale. . . . My work meant nothing if, while feeding me, it did not also make me part of something: pilot of a specific airline, gardener of a specific garden, architect of a specific cathedral, soldier of a specific country. If creating new airlines enriched us, it was because of the sacrifices that it demanded of us. The airlines were built with the free gift of our-selves. Once born, the airline gave us birth. If today I meet a comrade, I can say, "Do you remember . . . ?" It was a wonderful time when, bound by the same free gift of our-selves, we loved one another.

—Antoine de Saint-Exupery

We are the living links in a life force that moves and plays through and around us, binding the deepest soils with the farthest stars.

—Alan Chadwick
environmental gardener and visionary

Truth isn't always beauty, but the hunger for it is.

—Nadine Gordimer

Moral excellence comes about as a result of habit. We become just by doing just acts, temperate by doing temperate acts, brave by doing brave acts.

—Aristotle

Rely on the message of the teacher, not on his personality;
Rely on the meaning, not just on the words;
Rely on the real meaning, not on the provisional one,
Rely on your wisdom mind, not on your ordinary, judgmental mind.

—Buddha
The Four Reliances

The greatest achievements take the deepest patience and the longest time.

—Sogyal Rinpoche
The Tibetan Book of Living and Dying

Yes, risk-taking is inherently failure-prone. Otherwise, it would be called sure-thing-taking.

—Tim McMahon

Worrying is an insult to God.

—Source Unknown

If you bring forth what is within you, what you bring forth will save you. If you do not bring forth what is within you, what you do not bring forth will destroy you.

—Jesus Christ
The Gospel of Thomas

When you teach your son, you teach your son's son.

—The Talmud

A professional is someone who does his best work when he doesn't feel like it.

—Alistair Cooke

For me there is only the traveling on paths that have heart, on any path that may have heart. There I travel, and the only worthwhile challenge is to traverse its full length. And there I travel, looking, looking, breathlessly.

—Carlos Castenada
The Teachings of Don Juan

Call on God, but row away from the rocks.

—Indian saying

Just as iron rusts from disuse, even so does inaction spoil the intellect.

—Leonardo da Vinci

We still do not know one-thousandth of one percent of what nature has revealed to us.

—Albert Einstein

We are paradoxically restored to wholeness
as we surrender in defeat.

—Robin Norwood

I want my own will, and I want simply to be
    with my own will
as it goes toward action,
and in the silent, sometimes hardly moving
    times
when something is coming near,
I want to be with those who know secret
    things
or else alone.

—*Rilke*
from "A Book for the Hours of Prayer (#7)"

Doctors think a lot of patients are cured who have simply quit in disgust.

—Don Herold

Goals that are not written down are just wishes.

—*Famous saying*

A flicker of starlight, like a rainbow or a snowflake, is nature's way of granting wishes.

—Liesl Vazquez

Be yourself—who else is better qualified?

—Frank J. Giblin II

The proverb warns that, "You should not bite the hand that feeds you." But maybe you should, if it prevents you from feeding yourself.

—Thomas Szasz

The only people for me are the mad ones, the ones who are mad to live, mad to talk, mad to be saved . . . the ones who never yawn or say a commonplace thing, but burn, burn, burn, like fabulous yellow roman candles exploding like spiders across the stars.

—Jack Kerouac
On the Road

While there's tea, there's hope.

—Sir Arthur Pinero

I think that wherever your journey takes you, there are new gods waiting there, with divine patience—and laughter.

—Susan M. Watkins
American writer

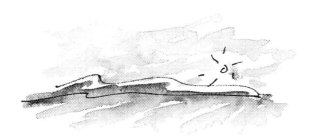

Nature uses as little as possible of anything.

—Johann Kepler

Where I was born and where and how I have lived is unimportant. It is what I have done with where I have been that should be of interest.

—Georgia O'Keeffe

Just to be is a blessing. Just to live is holy.

—Rabbi Abraham Heschel
I Asked for Wonder

Everybody can be great. Because anybody can serve. . . . You only need a heart full of grace. A soul generated by love.

—*Dr. Martin Luther King Jr.*

What you love is a sign from your higher self of what you are to do.

—Sanaya Roman
Living with Joy

Motivation is what gets you started. Habit is what keeps you going.

—*Jim Ryun*

It is easy to be independent when you've got money. But to be independent when you haven't got a thing—that's the Lord's test.

—Mahalia Jackson
gospel singer

You don't get harmony when everybody sings the same note.

—Doug Floyd
Spokesman Review

Give all that you have, it is the first step.

—Source Unknown

Hope is a feeling that you have that the feeling you have isn't permanent.

—Jean Kerr
Finishing Touches

There are two ways of spreading light: to be the candle or the mirror that reflects it.

—*Edith Wharton*

189

When something can be read without effort, great effort has gone into its writing.

—Enrique Jardiel Poncela

Dreams come true; without that possibility
nature would not incite us to have them.

—*John Updike*

$\mathcal{S}$oftness triumphs over hardness, feeble-ness over strength. What is more malleable is always superior over that which is immovable. This is the principle of control-ling things by going along with them, of mastery through adaptation.

—Lao-tzu

Only the man who can relax is able to create, and ideas reach his mind like lightning.

—*Cicero*

Fight on, my merry men all,
I'm a little wounded, but I am not slain;
I will lay me down for to bleed a while;
Then I'll rise and fight with you again.

—John Dryden

Our higher purpose is what we came here on a soul level to do. We are born with specific interests, talents, and abilities to fulfill that purpose.

—Shakti Gawain
The Path of Transformation

It is easy to sit up and take notice. What is difficult is getting up and taking action.

—Al Batt

The purpose of art is to lay bare the questions which have been hidden by the answers.

—*James Baldwin*

Everything is a miracle. It is a miracle that one does not dissolve in one's bath like a lump of sugar.

—Pablo Picasso

Never doubt that a small group of thoughtful, committed citizens can change the world. Indeed it is the only thing that ever has.

—Margaret Mead

I have come to realize that all my trouble with living has come from fear and small-ness within me.

—Angela L. Wozniak

Be thine own palace, or the world's thy jail.

—*John Donne*

Don't be agnostic—be something.

—Robert Frost

Life shrinks or expands in proportion to one's courage.

—Anais Nin
The Diary of Anais Nin

Patience, the essential quality of a man.

—Kwai-Koo-Tsu

Snowflakes are one of nature's most frag-
ile things, but just look what they can do
when they stick together.

—*Vista M. Kelly*

We should not look at or listen to the one we feel is making us angry and causing us to suffer. In fact, the main root of our suffering is the seed of anger in us. The other person may have said or done something unskillful or unmindful. But his unskillful words or actions arise from his own suffering. He may just be seeking some relief, hoping to survive. The excessive suffering of one person will very often overflow onto others. A person who is suffering needs our help, not our anger.

—*Thich Nhat Hanh*
The Blooming Lotus

Do but do.

—James Joyce

People with goals succeed because they know where they're going.

—Earl Nightingale

To know what you prefer, instead of humbly saying Amen to what the world tells you you ought to prefer, is to have kept your soul alive.

—Robert Louis Stevenson

Tradition lives because young people come along who catch its romance and add new glories to it.

—Michael Novak

The butterfly counts not months but
    moments,
And has time enough.

—Rabindranath Tagore

The intense desire for God realization is itself the way to it.

—Sri Anandamayi Ma

The most important thing a father can do for his children is to love their mother.

—*Theodore M. Hesburgh*

Though a tree grows ever so high, the falling leaves return to the root.

—*Malay proverb*

He who is afraid to ask is afraid of learning.

—*Danish proverb*

215

To be overpowered by the fragrance of flowers is a delectable form of defeat.

—Beverly Nichols
English writer

Inside myself is a place where I live all alone and that's where you renew your springs that never dry up.

—Pearl S. Buck

The elegance of honesty needs no adornment.

—Merry Browne

There are no menial jobs, only menial attitudes.

—William J. Bennett
The Book of Virtues

There is a magnet in your heart that will attract true friends. That magnet is unselfishness, thinking of others first. . . . When you learn to live for others, they will live for you.

—Paramahansa Yoganada

Every part is disposed to unite with the whole, that it may thereby escape from its incompleteness.

—Leonardo da Vinci

225

The less effort, the faster and more powerful you will be.

—*Bruce Lee*

You're young, you know a lot you won't know later on.

—Margaret Lawrence

Even if you're on the right track, you'll get run over if you just sit there.

—Will Rogers

The value of marriage is not that adults produce children, but that children produce adults.

—Peter De Vries
The Tunnel of Love

It is only when we become conscious of our part in life, however modest, that we shall be happy. Only then will we be able to live in peace and die in peace, for only this lends meaning to life and to death.

—Antoine de Saint-Exupery
Airman's Odyssey

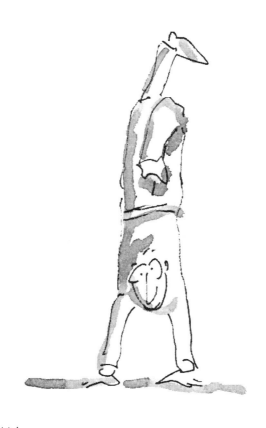

We all have talents one way or the other.

—Source Unknown

231

Always remember that if God had meant for today to be perfect he wouldn't have invented tomorrow.

—Source Unknown

When love and skill work together, expect a masterpiece.

—John Ruskin

Great qualities are too precarious when left to themselves, unsteadied and unballasted by knowledge, abandoned to mere impulse and untutored daring, they need the bridle as well as the spur.

—*Longinus*
On the Sublime

The sun will set without thy assistance.

—*The Talmud*

Give us grace and strength. Give us courage and gaiety and the quiet mind. Spare to us our friends and soften to us our enemies. Give us the strength to encounter that which is to come, that we may be brave in peril, constant in tribulation, temperate in wrath and in all changes of fortune, and down to the gates of death, loyal and loving to one another.

—Robert Louis Stevenson

Life is God's gift to you. The way you live it is your gift to God.

—Leo Buscaglia

S ervice is the rent we pay for our space on earth.

—*Russel Tompkins*
educational expert

The significant problems we face cannot be solved at the same level of thinking we were at when we created them.

—Albert Einstein

We carry with us the wonders we seek
without us.

—Sir Thomas Browne

Man can never be happy if he does not nourish his soul as he does his body.

—*The Rebbe*

Love turns work into rest.

—St. Teresa of Avila

That is what learning is. You suddenly understand something you've understood all your life, but in a new way.

—Doris Lessing

A wounded deer . . . leaps highest.

—Emily Dickenson

Soon after a hard decision something inevitably occurs to cast doubt. Holding steady against doubt usually proves the decision.

—R. I. Fitzhenry

A man is rich in proportion to the things he can afford to let alone.

—Henry David Thoreau

Character is that which can do without success.

—Ralph Waldo Emerson

247

No one can see his reflection in running water but only in still water. Only that which is itself still can bring stillness to all who seek after stillness.

—D. Howard Smith
The Wisdom of the Taoists

In Chinese, the word for crisis is wei ji, composed of the character wei, which means danger, and ji, which means opportunity.

—Jan Wong

Humor is not a trick, not jokes. Humor is a presence in the world—like grace—and shines on everybody.

—Garrison Keillor

To know and to act are one and the same.

—Samurai maxim

251

A sense of shame is not a bad moral compass.

—Colin Powell
My American Journey

If it's working, keep doing it.

If it's not working, stop doing it.

If you don't know what to do, don't do anything.

—medical school advice

Behold the turtle. He makes progress only when he sticks his neck out.

—*James Bryant Conant*

An apology is the superglue of life. It can repair just about anything.

—Lynn Johnston

All curiosity is at an end after Jesus, all research after the Gospel. Let us have Faith and wish for nothing more.

—*Tertullian*

If you haven't any charity in your heart, you have the worst kind of heart trouble.

—Bob Hope

Each thing we see hides something else we want to see.

—René Magritte

No steam or gas ever drives anything until it is confined. No Niagara is ever turned into light and power until it is tunneled. No life ever grows great until it is focused, dedicated, disciplined.

—*Harry Emerson Fosdick*

You cannot hold back a good laugh any more than you can the tide. Both are forces of nature.

—William Rotsler

Nothing great was ever achieved without enthusiasm.

—Ralph Waldo Emerson

Look at everything as though you were seeing it either for the first or last time. Then your time on earth will be filled with glory.

—Betty Smith
A Tree Grows in Brooklyn

The art of living is more like wrestling than dancing.

—Marcus Aurelius

It is better to be boldly decisive and risk being wrong than to agonize at length and be right too late.

—Marilyn Moats Kennedy

Here is the test to find whether your mission on earth is finished: if you're alive, it isn't.

—Richard Bach

I think and think for months and years.
Ninety-nine times, the conclusion is false.
The hundredth time I am right.

—*Albert Einstein*

Don't die before you're dead.

—title of a novel by Y. Yevtushenko

273

Man is a creature of hope and invention, both of which belie the idea that things cannot be changed.

—Tom Clancy
Debt of Honor

The less you open your heart to others, the more your heart suffers.

—Deepak Chopra
Ageless Body, Timeless Mind

While intelligent people can often simplify the complex, a fool is more likely to complicate the simple.

—Gerald W. Grumet, M.D.

We ourselves feel that what we are doing
is just a drop in the ocean. But the ocean
would be less because of that missing drop.

—Mother Teresa

The truth of the matter is that you always know the right thing to do. The hard part is doing it.

—Gen. H. Norman Schwarzkopf

If you're going to be able to look back on something and laugh about it, you might as well laugh about it now.

—Marie Osmond

In the midst of great joy, do not promise anyone anything. In the midst of great anger, do not answer anyone's letter.

—Chinese proverb

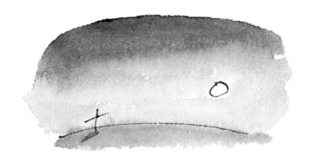

Jesus was all virtue, and acted from impulse, not from rules.

—William Blake

Happiness can be thought, taught, and caught—but not bought.

—Source Unknown

The worst prison would be a closed heart.

—Pope John Paul II

283

There are no short cuts to any place worth going.

—*Source Unknown*

The highest love of all finds its fulfillment not in what it keeps but in what it gives.

—*Source Unknown*

I can't go on, I'll go on.

—Samuel Beckett

All sunshine makes a desert.

—*Arabic proverb*

287

If you are to be, you must begin by assuming responsibility.

—Richard Bach

The sky is the daily bread of the eyes.

—Ralph Waldo Emerson

289

To fulfill a dream, to be allowed to sweat over lonely labor, to be given a chance to create, is the meat and potatoes of life. The money is the gravy.

—Bette Davis
The Lonely Life

Be faithful to that which exists nowhere but in yourself.

—André Gide

There is no greatness where there is no simplicity, goodness and truth.

—Leo Tolstoy

The greater the ignorance, the greater the dogmatism.

—Sir William Osler, M.D.

You can't help getting older, but you don't
have to get old.

—George Burns

Faith consists in believing when it is beyond the power of reason to believe. It is not enough that a thing be possible for it to be believed.

—*Voltaire*

Be gentle and patient with people. Everybody's bruised.

—Katie Lambert

Depression is the inability to construct a future.

—*Rollo May*

You are all you will ever have for certain.

—June Havoc

The point of therapy is to get unhooked, not to thrash about on how you got hooked.

—Maryanne Walters

There are 40 kinds of lunacy, but only one kind of common sense.

—*African proverb*

Speak to the earth, and it shall teach thee.

—Job 12:8

They laughed at Joan of Arc, but she went right ahead and built it anyway.

—*Gracie Allen*

Kindness is more important than wisdom,
and the recognition of this is the beginning
of wisdom.

—*Theodore Isaac Rubin, M.D.*
One to One

303

Often the best way to win is to forget to keep score.

—*Marianne Espinosa Murphy*

Everything comes to he who hustles while he waits.

—Thomas A. Edison

There are two kinds of people: the ones who need to be told and the ones who figure it out all by themselves.

—*Tom Clancy*
Without Remorse

It's impossible to overestimate the unimportance of most things.

—John Lange

The reputation of a thousand years may
be determined by the conduct of one hour.

—Japanese proverb

The most valuable work you do may be done in as little as five seconds to five minutes. A higher vantage point, a brilliant idea, a key change in habit, a break from pressure, a boost in metabolism or a pivotal decision can produce significant, lasting benefits.

—P. M. Senge
The Fifth Discipline

Make haste slowly.

—Zen master

A man is a god in ruins. When men are innocent, life shall be longer, and shall pass into the immortal as gently as we awake from dreams.

—Ralph Waldo Emerson

The worst bankrupt in the world is the person who has lost his enthusiasm.

—H. W. Arnold

Say what you have to say, not what you
ought.

—Henry David Thoreau

Life, like a dome of many-colored glass,
stains the white radiance of eternity.

—Source Unknown

314

To laugh often and much, to win the respect of intelligent people and the affection of children; to leave the world a bit better, to know even one life had breathed easier because you had lived; that is to have succeeded.

—Ralph Waldo Emerson

Fortune and misfortune are the result of our actions. Reward and retribution follow us like shadows.

—Lao-tzu

There is no situation, however seemingly hopeless or terrible, such as a terminal disease, which we cannot use to evolve. And there is no crime or cruelty that sincere regret and real spiritual practice cannot purify.

—Sogyal Rinpoche

When all the blandishments of life are gone, the coward sneaks to death, the brave live on.

—George Sewell

We know the truth, not only by the reason, but also by the heart.

—Blaise Pascal (1632-1662)

Great art can communicate before it is understood.

—T. S. Eliot

Sooner murder the infant in its cradle
than nurse unacted desires.

—*William Blake*

The most important of my discoveries have been suggested to me by my failures.

—Sir Humphrey Davey

Although we have been made to believe that if we let go we will end up with nothing, life itself reveals again and again the opposite: that letting go is the path to real freedom.

—Sogyal Rinpoche
The Tibetan Book of Living and Dying

Don't be afraid to take a big step if one is indicated. You can't cross a chasm in two small jumps.

—David Lloyd George

What one has to do usually can be done.

—Eleanor Roosevelt

Life has a practice of living you, if you don't live it.

—*Philip Larkin*

Although the world is full of suffering, it is full also of the overcoming of it.

—Helen Keller

Even a worm an inch long has a soul half an inch.

—*Buddhist proverb*

Job? A job? Who's talking about a job? I'm talking about a move, man.

—Eric Roberts in
The Pope of Greenwich Village

If your mind is empty, it is always ready for anything, it is open to everything. In the beginner's mind there are many possibilities, in the expert's mind there are few.

—Suzukiroshi

Nothing in human life, least of all in religion, is ever right until it is beautiful.

—Harry Merson Fosdick

331

It takes a long time to become young.

—Pablo Picasso

Of all modern notions, the worst is this: that domesticity is dull. Inside the home, they say, is dead decorum and routine; outside is adventure and variety. But the truth is that the home is the only place of liberty, the only spot on earth where a man can alter arrangements suddenly, make an experiment or indulge in a whim. The home is not the one tame place in a world of adventure; it is the one wild place in a world of rules and tasks.

—G. K. Chesterton

Any people anywhere, being inclined and having the power, have the right to rise up and shake off the existing government and form a new one. This is a most valuable and sacred right—a right which we hope and believe is to liberate the world.

—Abraham Lincoln

A good meal makes a man feel more charitable toward the whole world than any sermon.

—Arthur Pendenys

People love to talk but hate to listen. Listening is not merely not talking, though even that is beyond most of our powers; it means taking a vigorous, human interest in what is being told us. You can listen like a blank wall or like a splendid auditorium where every sound comes back fuller and richer.

—Alice Duer Miller

We act as though comfort and luxury were the chief requirements of life, when all that we need to make us really happy is something to be enthusiastic about.

—Charles Kingsley

Normal day, let me be aware of the treasure you are. Let me learn from you, love you, savor you, bless you before you depart. Let me not pass you by in quest of some rare and perfect tomorrow. Let me hold you while I may, for it will not always be so. One day I shall dig my nails into the earth, or bury my face in the pillow, or stretch myself taut, or raise my hands to the sky, and want, more than all the world, your return.

—Mary Jean Irion

Look up and not down
Look forward and not back
Look out and not in
Lend a hand

—Edward Everett Hale (1822-1909)
American clergyman

Our strength is often composed of the weakness we're damned if we are going to show.

—*Mignon McLaughlin*

We must become aware that all is mind: pain and pleasure, birth and death. Once this is truly seen, the conjurer can no longer function. The mind abandons its assumptions. And what's left over is Truth.

—Jacquelyn Small
Awakening in Time

Without the transcendent and the transpersonal, we get sick . . . or else hope-less and apathetic. We need something bigger than we are to be awed by and to commit ourselves to.

—Abraham Maslow

The source of all power is within yourself. Although external circumstances may occasionally hamper you, true movement comes solely from within yourself. The source is latent in everyone, but anyone can learn to tap it. When this happens, power rises like a shimmering well through the center of your body.

—Deng Ming-Dao
365 Tao

A person who is not disturbed by the incessant flow of desires—that enter like rivers into the ocean, which is ever being filled but is always still—can alone achieve peace, and not the man who strives to satisfy such desires.

—*Bhagavad Gita*

Of a certainty the man who can see all creatures in himself, himself in all creatures, knows no sorrow.

—Eesha Upanishad

Every moment of your life is infinitely creative and the universe is endlessly bountiful. Just put forth a clear enough request, and everything your heart desires must come to you.

—Shakti Gawain
Creative Visualization

Man cannot discover new oceans until he has courage to lose sight of the shore.

—*Source Unknown*

If we are a truly responsible person, we see clearly that we are accountable only for the foreseeable results of our own choices and actions—not for what other people feel, think or do.

—*Christopher J. McCullough, Ph.D.*
and Robert Woods Mann
Managing Your Anxiety

Remain calm, serene, always in command of yourself. You will then find out how easy it is to get along.

—Paramanhansa Yogananda

What is to give light must endure burning.

—Viktor Frankl

The main reason for healing is love.

—Paracelsus (1493–1541)

Pray as you can, not as you can't.

—Dom Chapman

Seek not abroad, turn back into thyself for in the inner man dwells the truth.

—St. Augustine

Nothing under heaven can arrest the progress of the human soul on its long pilgrimage from darkness to light, from the unreal to the real, from death to immortality, and from ignorance to wisdom.

—The Tibetan

354

I say these powers will be given to you, but more correctly, you give them to yourself, for you even now possess them though you know it not; nothing can be added from without, all comes from within.

—Will Garver

Feel the mystic light spreading silently
over your body, over trees, over vast lands.
. . . Behold the universe as Light.

—Paramanhansa Yogananda

356

Whatever you can do or dream you can, begin it. Boldness has genius, magic and power in it. Begin it now.

—Goethe

So who can be still and watch the chess game of the world?

The foolish are always making impulsive moves, but the wise know that victory and defeat are decided by something more subtle.

They see that something perfect exists before any move is made.

—*Brian Walker*
Hua Hu Ching

A little boy can be paralyzed with fear when he is told there is a boogie man under his bed who is going to take him away. When his father turns on the light and shows him there is no boogie man, he is freed from fear. The fear in the mind of the boy was as real as if there really was a boogie man there. He was healed of a false thought in his mind. The thing he feared did not exist. Likewise, most of your fears have no reality. They are merely a conglomeration of sinister shadows, and shadows have no reality.

—Dr. Joseph Murphy
The Power of Your Subconscious Mind

Only connect.

—E. M. Forster

To show a child what once delighted you, to find the child's delight added to your own—this is happiness.

—J. B. Priestley

You must speak straight so that your words may go like sunlight to our hearts.

—Cochise of the Apaches

Never let work drive you, master it and keep in complete control.

—Booker T. Washington

We must use time creatively, and forever realize that the time is always ripe to do right.

—Nelson Mandela

364

The earth's distances invite the eye. And as the eye reaches, so must the mind stretch to meet these new horizons. I challenge anyone to stand with autumn on a hilltop and fail to see a new expanse, not only around him, but in him, too.

—Hal Borland

Everyone has a mass of bad work in him which he will have to work off and get rid of before he can do better—and indeed, the more lasting a man's ultimate good work, the more sure he is to pass through a time, and perhaps a very long one, in which there seems very little hope for him at all. We must all sow our spiritual wild oats.

—Samuel Butler
The Way of All the Flesh

About the Artist

Richard Torregrossa is a journalist and illustrator who has freelanced for *Cosmopolitan, Self, Vogue, Ladies' Home Journal, Sassy,* and other national and regional publications. Born in New York City, he now lives in San Diego, California, where his work has received regional gallery showings. He is currently at work on a series of illustrated children's books. *The Little Book of Wisdom* is his first book.

Two New Collections of Single-Serving-Sized
Chicken Soup for the Soul™ Stories

A Cup of Chicken Soup for the Soul™

Jack Canfield, Mark Victor Hansen and Barry Spilchuk

With this collection of brand-new two-page stories, you can now enjoy fresh *Chicken Soup for the Soul* whenever you have a few spare moments. *A Cup of Chicken Soup for the Soul* is the perfect gift book for readers who loved the original *Chicken Soup for the Soul* or anyone looking for a quick pick-me-up.

Code 4215 . . . . $8.95

Condensed Chicken Soup for the Soul™

Jack Canfield, Mark Victor Hansen and Patty Hansen

Canfield, Hansen and Hansen have concentrated the very best short stories from *Chicken Soup for the Soul*, *A 2nd Helping of Chicken Soup for the Soul* and *A 3rd Serving of Chicken Soup for the Soul* in this delectable little volume. Whether you use it as a bedside companion or pocketbook reader, you'll love this small treasure.

Code 4142 . . . . $8.95